LIFE ON A GOAT FARM

LIFE ON A
GOAT
FARM

by Judy Wolfman
photographs by David Lorenz Winston

Carolrhoda Books, Inc. / Minneapolis

My thanks to the Search family for sharing their lives with me and providing me with information for this book; to the American Dairy Goat Association for supplying me with excellent additional material; and to Linda Spahr of the York County Extension Service for willingly answering my questions and concerns.   —J.W.

Special thanks to Leslie, Jimmy, Dean, and Lucas Search for the cooperation, patience, and hospitality they showed me while I photographed their beautiful farm.   —D.L.W.

Carolrhoda Books, Inc.
A division of Lerner Publishing Group
241 First Avenue North
Minneapolis, MN 55401 U.S.A.

Website address: www.lernerbooks.com

LIBRARY OF CONGRESS CATALOGING-IN-PUBLICATION DATA

Wolfman, Judy.
     Life on a goat farm / by Judy Wolfman ; photographs by David Lorenz
Winston.
          p.   cm.—(Life on a farm)
     Includes index.
     ISBN 1-57505-515-5 (lib. bdg. : alk. paper)
    1. Goats—Juvenile literature. 2. Dairy farms—Juvenile literature.
[1. Goats. 2. Dairy farms.] I. Winston, David Lorenz, ill. II. Title. III. Series.
SF383.35.W66 2002
636.3'9142—dc21   00-010226

Manufactured in the United States of America
1 2 3 4 5 6 – JR – 07 06 05 04 03 02

CONTENTS

Lots of **KIDS** Live Here

Can you guess who my brothers and I play with when our friends aren't around? Goats! My name is Jimmy Search, and I live on a dairy goat farm with my younger brothers, Dean and Luke. We have an older brother, too. His name is Mickey. He's in college, so he isn't home very much.

Our farm is called Lahaway Creek-Little Way Farm. We have almost one hundred goats. Our dad works for the state government. He travels a lot, so Mom does most of the farmwork. Dean, Luke, and I help her as much as we can on weekends and when we're off from school.

My little brothers and I like to play with our goats. I'm on the left hugging one of my favorites.

On a dairy goat farm, people keep goats for their milk. There are six kinds of dairy goats in the United States, and we have them all. My favorite is the Saanen. Saanens are big goats with short, white hair. They give a lot of delicious, creamy milk. Mom calls them her gentle giants because they're so easy to work with. We also own Alpine, LaMancha, Nubian, Oberhasli, and Toggenburg goats.

Saanens are all white.
Some people think that makes them boring, but I like them.

Rosalee is a LaMancha.
These goats can be combinations of black, brown, white, or red. Their ears are so tiny that some people think they don't have ears at all!

Vera is one of our Alpines.
Lots of people like Alpines because of their many colors. They have lots of personality, too.

We have one Nubian goat. I like the way its long ears hang way down.

Oberhaslis are reddish-brown with black legs and a black stripe down their back. They're not as big as other kinds of goats.

We also have one Toggenburg goat. It's brown with brown and white legs.

Most of these goats are Saanen does.

Since a girl goat, or **doe**, is the kind that makes milk, most of our goats are does. A doe gives milk only after she has a baby. That means we have to **breed** our does to make sure they have babies every year. We have two **bucks**, or boy goats, that we use for breeding.

It's easy to tell when a doe is in **heat**. (That's the time when she's ready to get pregnant.) A doe in heat acts goofy. She does lots of silly things, like wiggling her tail to get a buck's attention. She also hangs out by the gate to the pasture, where the bucks are kept.

When several does are in heat, Mom puts the bucks in two pens. She lets the does go in, and the bucks breed them to make them pregnant.

12

The bucks are separated from the does until breeding time. Many goat farms have just one or two bucks for breeding.

13

Patience has just given birth to her second kid. Since a lot of does are bred at the same time, we've had as many as eight kids born in one day. That's a lot of babies to care for!

About five months later, the doe is ready to give birth. She goes off by herself. Then she digs into the ground, lies down, and stands up, over and over. When we see a purplish-black bubble hanging out of her back end, we know the baby will be born soon. We wait close by and keep an eye on the doe, just in case she has trouble.

A few minutes later, the doe **freshens**, or has the baby. A baby goat is called a **kid.** Most of the time, the kid's front feet come out first. Next come the head and the rest of the body. If the kid doesn't come out as quickly as it should, we help Mom pull it out. Then we keep watching because another kid may be born. A doe usually gives birth to two kids at a time, though some does have only one. We've had fifteen goats that had three babies, or triplets. Two of our goats have had quadruplets—four babies at one time!

14

Newborn kids are a lot cuter after the mother licks off the mucus.

When a kid is born, its eyes are open and its tiny ears stand up straight. Its body is covered with short hair and a wet, slimy substance called **mucus**. The doe licks the kid to clean the mucus from its nose and mouth. If the weather is cold, we help dry the kid off with a towel. We make sure the kid's nose and mouth are clean so it can breathe.

A newborn kid stands 1 to 1½ feet tall and weighs 5 to 10 pounds.

Mom puts iodine
on a kid's belly.

The **umbilical cord** usually breaks as the baby is born. The umbilical cord is like a lifeline. While a kid is growing inside its mother, it gets food and oxygen through the cord. When the cord breaks, a small piece is left behind on the kid's stomach. We put iodine on it so it won't get infected. In about a week, the rest of the cord drops off. (Human babies have an umbilical cord, too. A person's belly button is the spot where the cord was attached.)

A kid gets its first vitamin shot.

We also give the kid four shots. Two are vitamins, and two help keep the kid from getting sick. Mom grabs the kid by the scruff of its neck and gives it two shots under the skin. The other two shots go into the kid's back leg. The shots don't seem to hurt, and they sure help the kid get off to a good start.

18

We watch to make sure the kid latches on to the mother's **teat** and starts **nursing**, or drinking milk. Before the doe produces milk, she makes a special liquid called **colostrum**. Colostrum is loaded with all kinds of good stuff that keeps the kid healthy. It's very important for the baby to get it soon after it's born. After the kid starts nursing, Mom milks the doe a little. She freezes some colostrum in case something happens to the doe and the kid can't nurse.

This kid is already a pro at nursing. Goats that have been bottle-fed are easier to sell as pets since they're friendly and used to being handled.

Some newborn kids are wobbly. It takes a while for them to stand up and nurse. But some can stand just ten minutes after birth. It's funny to see the kids stand, then fall. Every minute they get steadier on their feet. In a few hours, they're running around and jumping.

Patience helps her kid take its first wobbly step.

Luke bottle-feeds a kid whose mother is sick and can't nurse it.

Because our farm is a dairy, we don't keep many kids. We need to milk the does instead of letting the kids drink the milk. So most of our kids are sold two or three days after they're born. (Their new owners feed them with bottles.) We do keep a few kids, though. The boy kids will be sold for pets or for meat when they get bigger. The girls will grow up, have babies, and give milk like their moms.

This kid hasn't been dehorned yet.

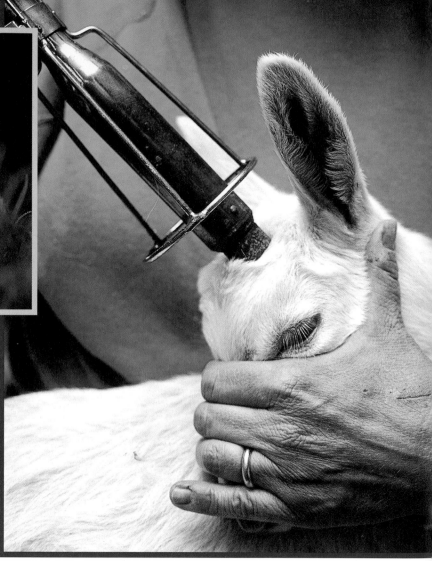

Mom uses a special tool to dehorn the goats.
Most kids are born with horns. We need to burn them off so the kids don't hurt each other.

Most goats, both boys and girls, are born with horns. If they keep their horns, they can hurt each other and us when they play. So we **dehorn** most kids when they're several days old. Mom burns off the horns with a tool called an electric disbudder. Since horns don't grow back, we only have to dehorn the goats once. A few kids are **polled**, which means they're born without horns. They don't have to be dehorned at all.

22

When a kid is two weeks old, we give it solid food pellets. The pellets are made of ground-up grains, seeds, and blackstrap molasses. The kids also keep nursing for three to four months. Then they're **weaned**—we don't let them nurse anymore. Once we had a kid that didn't like being weaned at all. It jumped over a fence, found its mom, and started nursing again!

This kid is still too young to be weaned from its mother.

Luke and I offer a baby kid its first solid food pellets.

Kids are very friendly and affectionate.

Kids are lots of fun to play with. My brothers and I like to play tag and run races with them. Sometimes a kid and I push each other, sort of like a wrestling match. But I'm always careful not to play too roughly.

Most goat farmers give their goats numbers, but we give ours names. If we don't recognize a goat, we look at the name tag hanging from its collar. But as the goats grow, we learn to tell them apart by their markings or eye color. Goats have many eye colors: black, brown, hazel, even blue or green.

By the time a kid is a year old, it's not a baby anymore. It's a doe or a buck. Once a doe freshens and becomes a mom, she's definitely an adult. Her milk comes in after her kid is born. Then she's ready to go to work for us—and that means being milked.

Here I am playing with a Saanen doe.

This Alpine goat, Babette, has brown eyes.

25

MILK for Everyone

We milk our does two times a day—in the morning and again at night. First we bring them into the milking room in the barn. Each doe is put into a headlock that goes around her neck. This headlock keeps the doe in place while she's milked, but she can move her head around and reach her food. The goats eat while they're being milked. That keeps them busy.

Luke locks the goats in for milking time.

The does eat from a feeder while they wait for their turn to be milked.

Goats have very flexible necks. Even in their headlocks, they can turn their heads easily.

It's important to keep the goats' udders clean and healthy so the goats are comfortable and can continue to produce milk.

I place the milking machine on a goat's teats. The milk is sucked into a large tank, where it's kept until it's packaged to be sold.

Before milking a goat, we wash her **udder** with a special liquid. (The udder is the part of a goat that makes milk.) Mom starts the milk flowing from each teat. She makes sure the milk looks good and isn't lumpy or stringy. Then we attach the milking machine to both of the goat's teats.

28

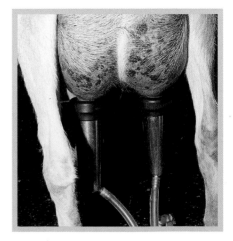

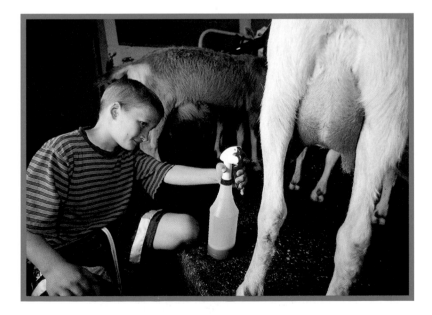

The milk is sucked up into a pipe called a milk line. It goes through a filter and into a big, cold holding tank. A paddle stirs the milk to keep it from sitting too long and turning sour.

Each goat gives milk for about four minutes. After a goat has been milked, we spray the end of her teats with teat dip. This keeps the udder clean and healthy. Then we bring the goat back into the main part of the barn or to the pasture.

Later Mom strains the milk into cans and takes it to the dairy. The man at the dairy pumps the milk through a machine. The machine heats the milk to a high temperature to kill any germs. Then it's cooled and put into bottles. Mom picks up the bottles, puts her label on them, and delivers them to nearby stores.

Being able to drink goat's milk is one of the best parts of having dairy goats. The milk is white and sweet and healthy. Goat's milk is easier to digest than cow's milk. It's also helpful for people who have allergies and other health problems. Mom says that around the world, more people use milk from goats than any other animal.

Mom takes the milk to a dairy to be bottled. Most of our milk is sold in stores, but sometimes people come to our house to buy it.

We don't just drink our milk—we also use it to make other foods. Butter isn't easy to make, but it's very good. And goat cheeses are great! Mom makes her own ricotta cheese for lasagna and calzones. If we smell vinegar in the house when we come home from school, we're excited because we know she's making ricotta. She makes delicious fudge with the milk, too.

But there's more to dairy goats than playing with them, milking them, and enjoying the foods we make from their milk. There's also an awful lot of work, every day of the week.

It's Not All PLAY

Owning goats is a big responsibility. Our animals depend on us for everything they need. For one thing, we have to make sure the goats are fed. Goats eat the hay and pellets we give them. They also eat grass, leaves, and plant stems in the pasture. A goat swallows its food quickly and stores it in its stomach for a while. Later the goat brings the food back up into its mouth and chews it again as **cud.**

Many people think goats will eat anything—even tin cans. But this isn't true. Goats are very fussy about their food. When a goat sees something new, it sniffs it and nibbles it a bit. But if the object is dirty or doesn't taste good, the goat will leave it alone. If a goat steps on its food, or if some hay falls from the rack, the goat won't eat it. But goats do eat paper, cigarettes, and Mom's plants and flowers.

Three thirsty goats drink from the fountain.

Goats eat grass and leaves in the pasture.

All the goats need mineral salt, baking soda, and fresh, clean water. If their stomachs get upset, they eat the baking soda. They get their water from an automatic fountain just outside the barn. When they go to drink, they knock each other out of the way because each one wants to be first. They're funny to watch.

33

Since goats eat a lot of grass, they need to be outside, free to walk around and graze. I love going into the field with them. They lean on me and sometimes nibble at my clothes. But they don't hurt me. When they all bleat at the same time, they're pretty noisy! Just like people, each goat has its own voice. Some are high, and some are low. Some say "baa," and some say "maa." They talk to each other, and sometimes they talk to me.

This bunch of goats can make the field a noisy place!

Both does and bucks have beards that have to be trimmed.

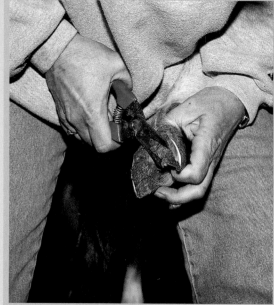

Mom trims a hoof so the goat can walk comfortably.

Luke and Dean brush the goats' coats so they stay clean and shiny.

Goat droppings look sort of like raisins. I don't like raking them up, but someone has to do it!

Goats need other kinds of care, too. Once a month, we use nippers to trim the goats' hooves. Goats have a **cloven hoof**, which means the hoof is split into two parts. If we don't trim them, the goats will be uncomfortable. We also trim each goat's beard. In the summer, when the goats are hot and dusty, we hose them down and give them a bubble bath.

The worst job is cleaning out the stalls where the goats sleep. Several times a week, Dean and I use a pitchfork to put a thick new layer of straw on top of the old stuff. The new layer holds in heat underneath it, so the goats stay warm in winter. Three times a year, Dad takes out all the old straw with a machine. Then he lays pine shavings on the barn floor and covers them with fresh straw.

This kid doesn't feel well, but it should be all right after a few hours in the house.

Just like people, goats sometimes get sick. But they're harder to doctor than people are. If a kid starts to look sick, we bring it into the house and put it in front of a heater. In two hours or so, it's usually okay. When an old doe gets sick, we do our best to help her get better. We give her some medicine and aspirin, keep her warm, and trim her feet to make her comfortable. Sometimes molasses in a bucket of hot water will give her a boost of energy and make her feel better. But if none of those things work, we can't let her suffer, so we have to send her to the meat man.

These Saanens are so excited to eat that they jumped in the feeder!

Goats are smart animals. Sometimes Mom takes a kid to school for show-and-tell. She takes the kid in our pickup truck, and it can figure out how to climb up the steps without any help! Some goats can be trained to pull a cart. But sometimes goats do dumb things, like trying to climb up on the hay bales and getting stuck between them.

Once I heard one of our goats, Madeline, yelling for help. Luke ran to her and saw that her foot was caught in the hayrack. It was twisted, and she couldn't get it out. Luke got Mom and Dad. When Mom pulled Madeline out, her leg was bent strangely. Dad pulled the leg and popped it back into the socket. Mom gave Madeline some pain medicine and held her for a while to make sure she was okay. We think Madeline was trying to jump over the hayrack but missed. After that, she never jumped again.

Since raising dairy goats is a full-time job, it's hard to take a vacation. Once in a while, a friend comes over to take care of the goats. Then we can go to the beach. But we don't mind staying home most of the time. Luke, Dean, and I like to play together. We play baseball, soccer, basketball, and football in nice weather. In the winter, we play in the snow. When we can't go out, we play games and read books inside. We all have schoolwork to do, too.

Dean, Luke, and I play little-league soccer and basketball at school,
so we practice a lot on the farm.

Goats have different ways of communicating with each other. These Nubian goats look like they're telling secrets.

These playful kids like to climb on the bales of hay in our barn.

When I grow up, I might be a goat farmer—or a math teacher or maybe even a veterinarian. Luke and Dean think they'd like to be goat farmers. Who knows? Maybe someday the three of us will run the farm and take care of Mom and Dad when they're older. I think they'd like that.

A dairy goat farm is a great place to live. I'm learning how to raise and care for goats and have fun at the same time. We have lots of space to run around and play in, and we have plenty of kids—the goat kind—to play with! I can't think of a better place to grow up.

Fun Facts about GOATS

Scientists who study the past believe that people first tamed goats more than 9,000 years ago in Asia.

What **important** product do you use **every day** in the **bathroom** that can be made from **goat's milk**? **SOAP!**

A goat's stomach has four different sections! The four sections allow the goat to digest tough foods that people can't digest, like grass.

In Mexico, people use goat's milk to make a delicious caramel called a *cajeta* (kah-HAY-tah).

There are more than 600 kinds of goats in the world! The pygmy goat, a relative of the dairy goat, is raised as a pet and for shows. A full-grown pygmy goat is less than 2 feet tall at the shoulder.

An adult buck can weigh 200 pounds or more — that's heavier than most adult people!

A doe gives as much as **A GALLON OF MILK** every day.

A doe usually freshens every year and lives about 13 years. If she has twins every year, she could have 26 kids in her lifetime!

BECAUSE GOATS LIKE TO EAT WEEDS AND BRUSH, SOME PEOPLE HIRE THEM TO CLEAN UP THEIR YARDS.

Learn More about GOATS

Books

Damerow, Gail. *Your Goats: A Kid's Guide to Raising and Showing.* Pownal, VT: Storey Communications, 1993. This detailed guide explores the different types of goats, their needs and behavior, and how to show a goat at a fair.

Morris, Ann. *700 Kids on Grandpa's Farm.* New York: Dutton Children's Books, 1994. Children discover how goats are raised and how goat milk is processed on their grandfather's farm.

Staub, Frank. *Mountain Goats.* Minneapolis: Lerner Publications Company, 1994. An introduction to the life cycle of the mountain goat, the wild cousin of the farm goat.

Websites

American Dairy Goat Association
<http://www.adga.org>
Here's a place for people who are serious about goats! Packed with information for farmers, this site also includes goat facts and a list of goat clubs. Follow the link in the "youth" section to find a recipe for goat's milk fudge.

Basic Goat Primer
<http://www.home.earthlink.net/~lureynolds/>
A goat fan surveys many kinds of goats, gives tips on how to raise healthy animals, and argues that goats are good for the environment.

Fias Co Farm
<http://www.fiascofarm.com>
The colorful home page of a dairy goat farm, this site includes a photo gallery, goat's milk recipes, and advice for farmers.

Goats and More Goats
<http://www.ics.uci.edu/~pazzani/4H/Goats.html>
Members of the Irvine Mesa Charros 4-H Club created this fun, informative site to share their knowledge of goats. Here you can read about the types of dairy goats, listen to the sounds they make, and play a goat game.

GLOSSARY

breed: to cause animals to mate and produce young. (The word *breed* also means to make pregnant.)

bucks: fully grown male goats

cloven hoof: a hoof that is split into two parts

colostrum: a liquid that a newborn goat drinks from its mother to help it stay healthy

cud: food that a goat brings up from its stomach to chew a second time

dehorn: to remove a goat's horns

doe: a fully grown female goat

freshens: gives birth

heat: the time when a female animal can become pregnant

kid: a baby goat

mucus: a slimy substance that covers a newborn goat

nursing: drinking milk from a mother's body

polled: born without horns

teat: a small, raised part on a mother goat's belly through which a young goat drinks milk

udder: the part of a female goat that makes milk

umbilical cord: the lifeline that connects a mother and baby while the baby grows inside the mother

weaned: not allowed to drink milk from a mother

INDEX

About the AUTHOR

Judy Wolfman is a writer and professional storyteller who presents workshops on creativity and storytelling. She also enjoys both acting and writing for the theater. Her published works include a children's play, numerous magazine articles, and Carolrhoda's Life on a Farm series. A retired schoolteacher, she has two sons, a daughter, and four granddaughters. She lives in York, Pennsylvania.

About the PHOTOGRAPHER

David Lorenz Winston is an award-winning photographer whose work has been published by *National Geographic World,* UNICEF, and the National Wildlife Federation. In addition to his work on the Life on a Farm series, Mr. Winston has photographed pigs, cows, and other animals for many years. He has also taught elementary school. In his spare time, he enjoys playing the piano at his home in southeastern Pennsylvania.